The First Lady's Manual

Home Is Where It All Begins

Vol 1

Latina C. Campbell

Copyright © 2021 Latina C. Campbell

All rights reserved. No part of this book may be reproduced in any form or by any electronic or mechanical means, including information storage and retrieval systems, without permission in writing from the publisher, except by reviewers, who may quote brief passages in a review.

ISBN: 9781735487182

Printed in the United States of America

Story Corner Publishing & Consulting, Inc.

1510 Atlanta Ave.

Portsmouth, VA 23704

Storycornerpublishing@yahoo.com

StoryCornerPublishing.com

Dedication

I want to dedicate this book to my Daddy, God. Without Him, I am NOTHING! Without Him, I would be in darkness. Lord, I thank you for saving me even when I tried to run away from you. You loved me even when I did not love myself.

I also dedicate this book to all the wives that diligently stand by their husband but get no recognition! Wives that are in the box, or the ones struggling to get out, this one is for you too! I promise you there is so much more to life when you live outside of the box.

Today is your day of freedom, no matter what they say or even what you think! You do not owe anyone an explanation to live, but it all starts with You.

Table of Contents

Scripture 1

Prayer 2

Introduction 4

Profile Rundown: Who Is She? 6

Problems Faced 18

Solution: What Does God Say? 28

Encouragement: Testimony of Overcoming 32

Serenity Prayer 35

Scripture

Theme Scripture:

"What therefore God has joined together, let not man separate."

Mark 10:9 ESV

Sub-scripture:

"Therefore, a man shall leave his father and mother and hold fast to his wife, and the two shall become one flesh."

Ephesians 5:31 ESV

Prayer

Dear Heavenly Father,

Thank you for being all that you are to us. Thank you for being so amazing, so kind, and so wonderful. You are The Most High God. You are ABBA, Father, the great shepherd, the healer, the restorer, the deliverer, the provider, the wonderful counselor, and much more. Thank you, God, for knowing just what we need and when we need it. You always come through on time. Hallelujah!!! You are holy and set apart from the rest. Nobody compares to you! Nothing compares to you! Lord, please forgive us for sins known and unknown in the name of Yeshua/ Jesus. Wash us white as snow Father. Holy Spirit sanctify us and help us to live holy and righteous in the sight of God. Lead us and guide us through the journey of life. Lord, I bind the spirit of religion, and I pray that it is broken off your people now in the name of Yeshua/ Jesus! I bind the spirit of Manipulation and Control, and I pray it is broken off your people now in the name of Yeshua/ Jesus. I bind the spirit of Witchcraft and pray it is broken off your people now in the name of Yeshua/ Jesus. Father, I lift every woman to you that You ordained as the wife of a ministry leader. I pray that you cover and keep them.

Show them who you created them to be and protect their marriage. I pray that you would rearrange marriages to mirror Christ and the church. I pray that you detach anyone from their union, causing discord in Yeshua/Jesus' name. I bind gossip, lies, addictions, sexual perversion, jealousy, envy, competition, adultery, and pride now in the name of Yeshua/ Jesus. I command it all to flee to the dry places now in the mighty name of Yeshua/ Jesus. I pray that You bind the wife and her husband together with cords that cannot be broken even by them. I pray you give them peace, joy, happiness, and prosperity. I even pray You keep them in good health. God, please reveal to the reader their purpose and show them how to achieve it. I pray that any woman reading this book will know that they are the apple of your eye and are genuinely loved by You. Show yourself to them when they feel alone and help them stand on Your Word even when times get rough! Take each woman deeper in You, God. Help them be the daughter, woman, wife, and even mother You have called them to be. Open their husband's eyes to see how you see them. Help the husbands always to cover, protect, and love their wives. Not my Will, but Your Will be done in Yeshua/ Jesus name Amen and Amen!

Introduction

Welcome to The First Lady's Manual. For starters, let us just set the record straight and address the elephant in the room! There is no such thing as a "First Lady" or a "First Lady's Manual." Yes, I know this is the name of my book, and we will get into that in a moment, but no one can tell you how to be YOU! The phrase "First Lady" is not biblical, so we need to stop using it. Also, no one can give you a manual on how to be a wife but God. God created us all differently, and He put in us what we need to be for our husbands.

Let us face it, "First Lady" is just a glorified title with no purpose given to a ministry leader's wife. This book teaches you not to be a wife or even how to be you; it will help you live outside of the box and remind you to seek God in all things. "The First Lady's Manual" is a collection of different struggles we face as wives of ministry leaders and how to overcome them.

For so long, wives were to be pretty trophies that sat quietly in the background, but today I say, NO MORE! It is time to pull back the covers to address the issues that have been and still are plaguing the leaders' wives. We have had to follow many made-up foolish rules of the "church" that God did not even set-in place, and we lost our identity in the process! We are instructed to be quiet and never have an opinion, so it does not affect our husbands' image. Just smile and pray, they say. We become invisible while making sure the spotlight shines bright on our husband. We transform into modern slaves under this made-up title of "First Lady." No

More! No More, I say!!! We have feelings, needs, and desires too. God has even given some of us visions, goals, and plans to follow. It is not just about our husband since the Word of God says the two shall become one flesh! My husband and I are one, so it is about us walking together side by side!

This series is to serve notice to the church and profess that enough is enough! Wives, be encouraged! You can make it through this. Stand up for what you believe in and be unshaken by what comes your way. I know it is Hell right now trying to make sense of it all, but when you walk in all of whom God has called you to be, it will all be worth it once you see the fruits of your labor.

Profile Rundown: Who Is She?

I remember like it was yesterday. My spiritual brother asked me to go to an installment service with him that would change my life forever! I have never been to an installment service before, so I did not know what to expect. I thought it would be a long boring service that would waste my time, and I did not want to go. I thought of graduation!! The most prolonged waste of time in history. Little did I know I was in for a surprise. Before I get into the installment service details, let me tell you a little about me and how I got to this point.

You see, I am not the typical born and raised church person. Yes, my grandmother took me a few times to church when I was a little girl, but I hated it because it was boring, and I felt better off doing something else! It just looked like a bunch of older people getting together, singing, and talking about people. I did not like the people at her church because I could see they were fake, and I spotted it when I walked into the building for the first time. Therefore, I did not go with her regularly. I just went to church to get out of the house. My house had a lot going on that drove me crazy, so I thought the church would be an escape, but I was wrong. I stopped going all together after an incident involving my younger sister occurred. She was getting bullied, and I would not allow it to continue once I found out. I never got the chance to get stuck in the tradition or routine of getting up and going to church just to go. I needed a purpose to do things, and since I did not receive it while going to church with my grandmother when I was younger, I took that into my adulthood. I just did not desire to go to church, nor was it a thought in my mind until years later with a mighty move of God. God made Himself known to me in a way I could not forget even if I wanted to.

Before the monumental installment service, God had a plan for me and a funny way of bringing it all together. How many of you know that there is nowhere for you to hide when you are in God's hands? Your purpose has a tracking device on you, and you will get to the finish line at your appointed time one way or another. My best friend, at the time, began going to church and enjoyed it. It was strange because she was not the typical "church" person either. Out of nowhere, she woke up one morning and wanted to go to church, so she did. She told me all about it periodically with great joy and even invited me to go with her. I could not wrap my mind around it because I just could not understand how she looked at "church" in such an embracive way. A part of me became curious to find out for myself what the rave was all about. What made this church so special? It took me a while to accept the invitation because of my church experiences, but her consistency motivated me to go. I trusted her as a reliable source, so I eventually went. When I finally got the courage to go, I met her Pastor as I walked into the door because he called me right up to the front of the altar. He was a Prophet, and I had no idea what a Prophet was at that time. When he started telling me my whole life, I knew there was something different about him. I had to give the side-eye expression to my best friend because I felt set up! At first, I thought she had told him these things about me until he went into secret places of my life that I did not even share with her!

At that point, I knew it was God. Only God knew those things about me because I would mumble them to myself at times. Yes, I spoke to myself a lot back then because I did not trust anyone with my extra personal business, and somehow, I needed to vent. I did not have a relationship with God, which would have enabled me to give Him my mess in prayer, so I had to hold it. As I would vent to myself, God was picking up every word and saving it for a time such as this. I did not have an intentional prayer life. I would randomly pray when I got into a negative life-changing mess that hung over my head. I only knew of God from the limited information the church people would share. I knew He created me and died for me, but that was it. I did not know all that He could do, but I would pray for help from Him. I had to be in a near-death experience to even talk to God because I did not think He could hear me. For some reason, I would still try to get through to Him. Since I did not go to church every Sunday, I thought that He did not want to hear my prayers. People would make it seem as if the church were God, and if I stayed away from the church, I was missing out on God. As I said, I would pray anyway for some reason.

Now, standing at the altar of my best friend's church where her Prophet/ Pastor read my life like a book, I was lost for words! Only God could have shown him all of me like that. I broke down, crying like a baby. I knew at that moment; God was listening to me all those times I thought I was alone, and He was answering my prayers despite what I thought about prayer, church, and even Him. So many emotions saturated me at once that I almost passed out! After that experience, God began to show Himself to me more and more each day! I continued to attend my best friend's church here and there because I realized there was so much to learn about God!

Let me fast forward a year or so to where I started a new job. God was even in that; little did I know at the time. God sent another Prophet to speak to me at work! Still, in shock from the last Prophet, I almost ran. He came off extra strong, and this message was different for me. He briefly told me about my life, then he offered me salvation, or shall I say, offered me a chance to be saved. I asked him what was I being saved from and why did I need to be saved? Why did getting saved matter? I was not a church person, so why did I have to do it? And why now? I did not have anything against God, but it seemed like a lot of effort had to go into it, and I did not want to do all of whatever it was. Not even sure why. I guess because I just did not understand it all then. The Prophet broke salvation down to me, and I was still trying to get away from being "saved" that night at work. I thought I had more time and that it was not urgent. God then spoke through him, saying this was my last chance or I would die in the world! Something about those words sent chills up my spine, and I became fearful. Those words penetrated my heart, and I knew it was time to surrender right then and there. I immediately started to think about my children and all the mess I was going through.

Who would raise my children if I were not around? The horror I was in felt like it was already starting to kill me, so I knew it was not a lie. I was stressed, depressed, and borderline suicidal already. I knew the Prophet was allowing God to use him because he did not know anything about me. That was our first night working together, even though we attended training together. We did not speak to each other like that then.

He reiterated that salvation was simply accepting Jesus Christ, the son of God, into my life. He said it was better to have Jesus and not need Him, versus needing Jesus and not having Him at all. I thought to myself, if getting "saved" was going to help me be around for my children, then I would do what I must do. I would do whatever it took for them. At that very moment, I surrendered myself FULLY over to God. I knew a change had come over me because I began to cry out tears of joy uncontrollably. It was like heat fell all over my body, but I did not break a sweat! After I accepted Jesus into my life, I knew something happened to me because I could feel it! I felt FREE! Something broke off me, and I felt like my wings were released to fly for the first time in my whole life! I felt like I could really fly, run a marathon, and even swim around the world.

I wanted to tell everyone about Jesus Christ so they, too, could feel the freedom I felt. After that night, the Prophet became my coach, mentor, counselor, prayer partner, and after a while, my Spiritual Brother! He challenged and motivated me to learn more about God, Jesus, and the Holy Spirit every day. He pushed me to pray and to study God's Word. God started to reveal much more to me that was not even in the pages of the Bible. I never knew God was so mysterious. I genuinely enjoyed learning about God. I began to seek God for my purpose in life. I wanted to know why He created me. Why did He choose me to accept salvation?

I could not thank my now spiritual brother enough for his obedience to God because I was not an easy case. He indeed left an imprint on my life forever. God knew what He was doing when He chose him to minister to me. I was now dedicated more than ever to church every Sunday to get even more teachings about God from the Prophet/ Pastor at my best friend's church. I had a drive out of nowhere to learn about God. I even shared with the Prophet/ Pastor at my best friend's church that I had accepted salvation! He congratulated me and let me know he had a message from God for me! God told him to release me from his ministry because the ministry God had for me was predicated upon where my husband would go. I said, WHAT?! Husband? Who husband? Because I have no husband! There was so much to take in at once!

First off, I just started going every Sunday, and now I get kicked out?? I was upset it happened when I finally got comfortable there. Secondly, I made up in my mind that I would give God my whole body, mind, and soul. I just surrendered all of me and needed to be covered in prayer by someone I could trust. I asked God to keep me until He sent me a husband, but I was delighted with only God in my life. I was in no rush for a husband! Lastly, I felt annoyed because I had to go to a church where "my husband." I did not want to think that he had control over where I learned about God! What if I did not like the church he was attending? Yes, I was that strong independent female that did not need anyone, and I barely listened to someone! It would almost kill me to even ask for help. Ha-ha. Do not judge me! It was sad how I became programmed that way because I was not always that way. Throughout my life, I was wronged more times than I could count, and it changed the way I viewed people.

A couple of days before the Prophet/ Pastor released me; my spiritual brother tried to get me to go to Bible study with this Lady Pastor that he knew. I did not want to go, so I pushed that conversation to the farthest part of my mind. Then, the Prophet/ Pastor gives this message to me about being released from his ministry?? I figured since the Prophet/ Pastor was kicking me out, and I had nowhere else to go, I had to find somewhere to go quick, so the fire I had for God did not die. I was not going back to my mother's or my grandmother's religious boring church after witnessing all churches were not the same! I needed somewhere to go that I could feel free to worship and talk to God!

I received a phone call from the Lady Pastor, and I was so surprised to feel welcomed through the phone call. My spiritual brother gave her my number to contact me because he knew I would not reach out to her. Since she took the initiative, I then agreed to attend her service that Sunday, and I was happy I did. I felt God in a whole new way! I felt like this was the place for me even though I fought my spiritual brother on it. I was still afraid to step out and join her ministry since everything was new. I could not let go of the church I was released from, so I decided to attend both services since the service times permitted. I went to the Prophet/ Pastor's service during the morning and the Lady Pastor's service in the evening. At some point, I had to choose because it was occupying my whole day, but I was not ready just yet. I needed God to show me a sign that only He could. In the process of waiting for a sign, everyone at the Lady Pastor's church was preparing for their installment service. My spiritual brother saw the installment flyer, and he wanted to attend to support his spiritual brother named Paul. I was shocked that he had such a deep relationship with someone from that church that he never mentioned to me, and we talked about several things. I did not know Paul at all. I would only hear him sing in church, and I could not wait for him to sit down. Ha-ha. Paul was one of the people to be installed as Pastor during the installment service.

As I stated at the beginning of this story, I did not want to go to the installment service, but my spiritual brother convinced me to go with him anyway. So, let us fast forward to the day of the installment service. I attended the service, and I even invited one of my sisters to come along with me. We arrived at the service, and to my surprise, it was not a boring service as I expected it to be. The service was something like I had ever experienced in my life! During that time of worship, something different happened to me! I heard the voice of God for the first time! I thought I had gone completely crazy and that it was time to check myself into a mental institution. I heard His voice crystal clear! I could not even pretend that I did not Him. It was the voice of a man! It was not loud, but it was loud enough for me to hear Him. It was not heavy, but it was firm and direct. The voice shook the insides of my body, and my ears became hot.

He did not say just one word, but three words! I knew it was none other than God himself!! Every part of my body knew it was God for some reason. I did not doubt it. As everyone was in worship, I told God that I would embrace whatever husband He had for me since He wanted me to be married. I felt like God was waiting for me to accept the husband He had for me to move in my life like never before. I was petitioning God for a few things, and none of them was a husband, but God wanted to add that to my list. I rejected it first, so I figured God dismissed my list of requests since I did not see the manifestation. The main thing I was concerned about God doing for me was to give me a brand-new house for my children and me. I figured if I had to accept the husband that God had for me to get the house, then so be it. I was a little nervous about the whole husband thing because I was over relationships at that point. I had just got out of one filled with violence that I thought I would end up killing him or the relationship itself would kill me. So, wanting another man right then was not on my mind, but I trusted that God knew best. In that moment of me surrendering to God's Will for my life, He spoke to me.

He said, "Paul." I said, "Paul?" He said, "Paul." I said, "huh??" As God was speaking to me, Paul was the one receiving his certificate from the Lady Pastor. The Lady Pastor began to give him encouraging words. She told him not to be afraid to share his testimony. The voice of God then said, "homosexuality." I realized God was telling me the name of my husband and that he dealt with homosexuality. I said, "God, now you know you wrong! How you going to do me like that??" I then prayed that God was referring to another Paul as my husband. I began to watch the church's front door at that moment, to see if the other Paul walked in. It could not have been the Paul at the alter receiving his certificate! I had to start laughing because God was funny on so many levels!

First, God revealed to me who my husband was, and he was not my type! Not saying he was not a nice guy, but no! I would choose the "other guy." I am sure that was why I went through so much Hell in all my past relationships because it was not who God wanted for me. I guess that is why I had to allow God to show me who He created for me. Second, God showed me I was going to be the wife of a Pastor! Like really God? God was making sure I would not backslide away from Him and the church if times got rough. He assigned me a Pastor to always hold me accountable.

Lastly, God revealed to me my husband's testimony was homosexuality? God, really? I was not nervous about the actual testimony because I used to sleep with women for a very brief part of my life, but I was a little afraid to question if he was entirely out of that lifestyle or not. I wanted to know if he was still fighting with letting it go, did he get delivered from it, or was he comfortable in the closet? I did not want to walk into a situation where I had to fight for my place or feel that his mind would not be with me because it was with someone I could never be. I had never been with a man with that type of testimony, so it was different for me. I wanted to know if I would have had to fight men and women or just men off him. Would he still look at men behind my back? Was he even going to be interested in me being as though men were his go-to fix? I just had so many questions for God, but overall, I had to trust that God knew what He was doing. Looking at Paul, I would have never guessed he used to be a homosexual. I just thought he dressed differently, or maybe it was a Philly thing because I was not from there. I usually could point it out right away since I played in that lifestyle for a little, but I could not see it on him.

That was the only thing that brought me some ease because I felt as if that was a sign that he left that lifestyle. I told God that He would have to send Paul to me since he is my husband. I was not going to him! The Word says, "He who finds a wife...," so I was standing firm on that. If Paul did not approach me and in a suitable time frame, I asked God to send me someone else, although I was kind of hoping Paul did not come forward. I was skeptical and nervous, but I did not want to wait forever to get married now that I knew who God picked for my husband. For so long, I made my own choices with no direction from God, and I decided on the men I wanted, only to be miserable with whom I chose. This time around, I was kind of excited and interested to meet the man that God created just for me. God is perfect in all His ways, so I knew God's Will was perfect for my life also. A few days later, unbeknownst to me, my spiritual brother gave Paul my number, and he reached out to me right away. I was so surprised and had to look up at God for a moment because He answered my prayer quickly! So many emotions raced through my mind as we texted back and forth. I could not believe it was happening, just how I asked God.

I asked God to send him to me, and He did. Paul asked me on a date and a couple of weeks after the date he proposed. God showed him that I was the wife he had been searching for for some time. I said," yes," of course, and about a week after that, we got married! I became Mrs. Campbell, or shall I say "Lady Campbell" for the church people. We both knew God chose us for each other, so there was no need to wait and prolong the process. What God says shall be no matter who approves of it or not!

Problems Faced

I fully embraced the Mrs. Campbell title, but I had a hard time welcoming "Lady Campbell." Yes, I accept that I am the Pastor's wife, but a conflict happened as I transitioned hats. I realized that the "church" people I was surrounded by had their own set of rules regarding how a leader's wife should be. They placed so much pressure on the wives to transform into something other than what God called them to be. It stressed me out, and I struggled in the beginning. Of course, I did not want to be an embarrassment to my husband, but most importantly, I did not want to embarrass myself or God. God sent me, so I was trying to make Him proud. I was new to the faith and was still learning God's Word, whereas others in the church were more "advanced" than I was. They looked down on me because I was "newly saved," and they thought I knew nothing. They felt as if my husband was better off with someone born and raised in the church. They wanted someone easy to manipulate and already conformed to the "church" ways.

I never was the type to be controlled or follow the crowd, so it was hard to conform to the church's ways—keyword church, not God. I know I am here to stand out because, for starters, I have God in my life, and I am no small woman. Mrs. Campbell knew who she was, but "Lady Campbell" had some soul searching to do. You see, I had a problem with following something that I knew was not right, but as the wife, I got beat over the head with the word submit a lot. When my husband and I got married, he was religious and had already conformed to the church ways of doing things. One way to be "religious" is to follow a set of rules or doctrine the church made up that God never set-in place. They are rules that seem suitable for us, but they are there to brainwash, control, and turn us away from God. It is a doctrine that points us to the church and not God. The church said I had to dress a certain way, walk a certain way, and talk a certain way when Jesus/ Yeshua only requested us to follow Him. They did not want me to speak at all in fear of what I might say. I have seen a lot and knew a lot, so they surely did not want me to reveal their schemes. They slipped a spiritual yoke around my neck, and they were using my husband to hold the chain. They used the one closest to me because they could have never accomplished that on their own. My husband would enforce specific rules at home but not follow them himself. He would continuously use The Word of God against me, pointing out scripture for the wife but would dismiss the ones the husband should follow. Our leader at the time even told me not to worry about what my husband did but to make sure I did what I had to as the wife. It did not help that our leader was my husband's mother because she babied and took up for him when he was wrong. She was biased, and I had to understand that. So, whatever I said went out of the window, and I was the one always wrong and needing to apologize. My husband would do and say things just to see how I would respond. When I did not respond to his liking, he would report it back to the church, and they would "preach" about it during Sunday service. After this happened a few times, I knew they were preaching about me. I would confront our leader about it, but she would always lie and say God led the message when it was my husband reporting to them. My husband and I would argue like cats and dogs because I knew what was going on, and I was not going to submit without a fight!

They wanted my husband to keep me in alignment at home with their rules, and then they would reinforce them in the church to make it believable. After a while, I started to think that what they were saying was right because they had me alone and surrounded by only their perspective. These were the beginning stages of brainwashing. You see, when the enemy attacks, he wants to hit targets that are easy for him. I started with a couple of mentors until my husband and our leader thought it would be best to let them go. I did not know that it was a plan to get me alone so they could try to manipulate me to think how they thought. They knew I did not have enough Word inside of me at that time to combat the lies they were throwing out, so I fell prey to them.

We must know the Word of God because that is the truth we should live by, and when we do not know the Word, we will be misled by the lie. When we use God's Word out of context or incorrectly, it is a lie. When we add or take away from God's Word, it is a lie. When we only use half of His Word, it is a lie. It is so easy to fall into the trap of the enemy by merely mishandling or lacking the Word of God. The Word of God is God, and God will not stand for us, abusing Him. It is also essential to go deeper in God every day. There is always something new to learn about God. When you have an ear to hear God, you will discern when something is not right. When the church would preach lies, I would suddenly feel sick during that service. I did not know what it was in the beginning until God revealed to me that His truth was not being released during those times.

I would be so furious with my husband because I knew he was born to lead and not follow. I knew my husband was not like them and just followed their lead to be accepted, but it hurt me in the process. I could see the tug-of-war that was going on inside of him, but he would not come to reality with it no matter what I said. I could not understand it until God showed me the yoke around my husband's neck and reminded me why He chose me. "And it shall come to pass in that day, that his burden shall be taken away from off thy shoulder, and his yoke from off thy neck, and the yoke shall be destroyed because of the anointing." Isaiah 10:27.

It is the anointing or the power of God that frees us from strongholds. God gave us power, love, and a sound mind, so I had to work that power He placed inside of me. They held my husband's chain so he could not see it, and he had no idea it was even there. My husband also trusted these people because they were family and so-called friends, so he did not even think to look for a chain. He was so far in; I knew only a mighty move of God would get him out. I had no idea that God wanted to use me to break the yoke off him! Focusing on what they were doing to me almost had me forfeited my assignment. They were trying to distract me just as the enemy does to us all every day. For my husband to be all that God intended him to be, he needed to be set free. Until my husband was set free, I would stand in the box of darkness at church and home. I began to fast and pray like a madwoman! It was all I knew to do. God would give me the revelation of scriptures that would blow my mind, so when I heard it in church preached incorrectly, it made me upset.

I started strong, fighting the good fight with ease until I took my eyes off God and focused on the people. I came down off the prayer wall giving Satan room to run rampant in my life. I was then tossed back and forward like the ocean waves among the church and my husband. I became weak, weary, and wanted to give up. I started praying less and less until I wanted nothing to do with it, including my marriage. I felt like my prayers were going unanswered, so what was the point? My husband and I elevated in arguing until it was all we did. There were even moments when we put our hands on each other. I knew something had to give at that point. I could not go on too much longer in my marriage like that. The "church" was controlling our marriage, and God was no longer the center of it all. The church turned my husband and me against each other by telling him one thing and telling me another, so when we came together, it was always a disagreement. When we would be in front of the people at church, we had to act like everything was good as they persecuted me. I even tried to stomach their made-up rules for my marriage's sake because I knew God would charge me if I had any blame in the matter! Little did I know fault came anyway every time I followed the church's rules and not God's. They said, as a wife, I was not supposed to voice my opinions. My opinions did not matter because it was all about what my husband had to say. Wives were not supposed to have a vision because it was the husband that gave them the vision. Wives were to trade in their relationship with God only to have one through their husbands. If our husband did not sign off on something, then it was not approved, no matter if God said it or not. They said wives did not hear from God since the husband is our head. Wives must submit to their husband's lead even if he did not follow Jesus/ Yeshua. Wives are only around to cater to their husband's needs. The church still viewed the wives as Eve back in the garden when she ate the fruit. They believed wives were deceitful, wicked, and sent to destroy their husbands. Therefore, wives had to be quiet and look pretty with their heads covered.

The wife's uniform was a loose dress or skirt with tight stockings and high heels. They better not have thought about wearing pants or sneakers to church. My husband and I got into so many arguments because of their dress attire alone. My husband saw the women in his family dress a certain way to attend church, so he thought I was supposed to dress that way as well. So much so that he would rush to buy me clothing, and they would be the same style his mother, our Apostle at the time, would wear. I did not want to seem ungrateful because he did take the time to buy me something, but he never considered my style before shopping for me. He would always compare me to his mother, and I could not be myself because I was not good enough for him when I did not size up to her in his eyes. I do not compare or compete with anyone, so I told him to leave me and marry his mother. I became angry, bitter, resentful, and mad at God for arranging my marriage with Paul. I felt as if I married the wrong Paul. I started hating my marriage, my husband, his family, and the church! Most of the church members were part of his family, so I had no way to escape them unless I went to another church!

Eventually, I did attend another church, or should I say I went back to my old church. I just could not tolerate all the lies, gossip, backstabbing, discord, and most importantly, I was over pretending everything was okay. Things were not good, and I was NOT OK! I had no one to talk to, and even when I tried to say something about the matter, God would have me to be quiet. I was ready to explode inside and even thought about blowing up the church with everyone inside, except myself, of course. Ha-ha. Well, that was a thought anyway until I felt God gave me the side-eye expression. Ha-ha. So much was going on behind closed doors that my husband and I had grown distant. We were roommates at home and the "couple everyone wanted to be like" in public until they noticed I stopped going to church with him. I had no idea that my husband's actions would affect us so much that I contemplated divorce. We were so happy to get married initially, but once we said, "I do," everything drastically changed! I was blown away by what religion and several other spirits were doing to our marriage. I was over it all.

I knew I had to sacrifice in my marriage, but I felt like I sacrificed so much that I forgot who I was after a while. I gave up the identity God gave me, trying to conform to the people's thoughts about me. I tried to play nice when I should have been sounding the alarm in prayer. I felt like I was just around as a trophy to look good on my husband's arm and that they would never receive me no matter what I did. I remembered the scripture Romans 12:2, "And be not conformed to this world: but be ye transformed by the renewing of your mind, that ye may prove what is that good, and acceptable, and perfect, will of God." I had to be okay with not fitting in because God did not want me to conform to their ways. Instead, I had to transform my mind, perspective, and the way I thought about things. The only way transformation could take place was through the Word of God, so I had to get back to His Word.

When I did not follow the church, they said I was rebellious, controlling, and labeled me a witch. It was almost like a cult that my husband belonged to, and when they found out that I could see clearly, they wanted me gone. The warfare was so great that I thought God left me at some point. I began to question my salvation. My thoughts were that a saved person should not have to go through the amount of Hell that I was experiencing. God revealed that persecution is what "saved" people go through because His son, Jesus/ Yeshua, went through it. They assassinated my character behind my back and changed how people would view me. They spread around the church that I was not saved and did not know God; therefore, people did not receive the mantle and title God placed on my life. They planted seeds of discord, which had other people turning away from me, not even wanting to get to know me. The kicker was they were strangers that pretended to know me. The people the church turned away did not even know me. They wanted me dead because the last thing they wanted was for my husband to break out of their spell! God revealed to me that he put my husband and me together to break generational curses.

I had no idea what God meant by that initially, but my eyes started to open quickly. My husband came from a lineage of religion, witches, and sexual perversion, to name a few. So, I went through a lot, just trying to stand on God's Word while drawing my husband with love and kindness. I felt like Bell in *Beauty and The Beast.* She had to break the curse off the beast placed on him by a witch who wanted him to see things her way. I did not realize how much work it was to fulfill the scripture "the two become one flesh" Mark 10:8. I felt we had so much "becoming" to do that it was merely impossible to accomplish. I would cry out to God daily asking Him why He paired me with this man. My husband did not want to cleave to me as his wife, nor did he put his kids and me first. The spell kept him out of alignment, cleaving to his mother instead, but the devil is a liar! I know we had a lot to learn about marriage and still do. We did not have any marriages before us that followed God's Word, but I did not think it should have been that hard to align with God, especially being leaders in the ministry.

Everyone was so quick to put the wives in a box. Half of them were miserable that it was not them in that spot, and the other half did not agree with the pick God chose. In the Bible, the people chose Saul to be king, but God put David in line to be king. David went on to become one of the greats in the position of a king. David was the least likely, according to the people, but he had a heart after God. David was dear to God. I reminded myself often that God predestined our marriage even before we were born, just as He did David's kingship, so it did not matter what the people said or what my husband did. I had to trust God with all my heart and trust that God's Word was true because His Word says He is not a man that He shall lie.

My husband was not all bad, but each situation piled together made him appear that way until God told me not to walk by sight. Every time I fought with my husband instead of fighting in prayer, I lost the battle. We must remember that there is always a spiritual war going on and the only way we can do damage is to pray against the plans of the enemy seeking to destroy marriage. According to Ephesians 6:12, "For we are not fighting against people made of flesh and blood, but against persons without bodies- the evil rulers of the unseen world, those mighty satanic beings and great evil princes of darkness who rule this world; and against huge numbers of wicked spirits in the spirit world." You see, there are evil spirits sent to work against God-ordained marriages. The enemy wants us to focus on each other, so we do not think that it is him controlling things behind the scenes. Satan hates unions that God put together because he knows when the two become one and obey God, there will be damage done to his plans. God puts together marriages to advance His Kingdom and to bring Him glory. Marriage is not even about the two in it. It is so much bigger! Allow God to open your eyes to see how He sees. I promise life would be so much easier.

Solution: What Does God Say?

The only way I overcame the box of the "First Lady" was to allow God into it. Inside of the First Lady box were lies, hurt, pain, jealousy, envy, manipulation, control, rebellion, anger, rage, identity crisis, bitterness, resentment, loss of dreams, loss of hope, blindness, etc. I can go on and on, but I will stop there. All these things dwell in the First Lady's box because either the people &/or the wife put them there. God does not want us miserable as wives because He is joy. If we have God in our lives, we have joy also. When we follow God instead of "the people," we will have a successful life and marriage.

Here are the guidelines God requires husbands and wives to follow in His Word: Ephesians 5:21-33 states, "Submit to one another out of reverence for Christ. Wives, submit yourselves to your own husbands as you do to the Lord. For the husband is the head of the wife as Christ is the head of the church, his body, of which he is the Savior. Now as the church submits to Christ, so also wives should submit to their husbands in everything. Husbands, love your wives, just as Christ loved the church and gave himself up for her to make her holy, cleansing her by the washing with water through the word, and to present her to himself as a radiant church, without stain or wrinkle or any other blemish, but holy and blameless. In this same way, husbands ought to love their wives as their own bodies. He who loves his wife loves himself. After all, no one ever hated their own body, but they feed and care for their body, just as Christ does the church— for we are members of his body. "For this reason a man will leave his father and mother and be united to his wife, and the two will become one flesh." This is a profound mystery—but I am talking about Christ and the church. However, each one of you also must love his wife as he loves himself, and the wife must respect her husband." Amen.

This scripture is the secret or blueprint to a happy marriage! This operation is failproof because God's name is on it. It is His Word that will not return to Him void, meaning unfulfilled. Jeremiah 29:11 states, "For I know the plans I have for you, declared The Lord, plans to prosper you and not to harm you, plans to give you hope and a future." God wants us to prosper, even in marriage. The Word of God is clear, but people will pick and choose which scripture they want to follow and which scripture they do not. It is all or nothing with God. God wants us hot or cold for Him; there is no space in between. God also wants us to love each other as He loves us. "For God so loved the world that He gave His one and only Son, that whoever believes in Him shall not perish but have eternal life." John 3:16

God's love is entirely different from the world's love, and it took me some time to understand that. Love covers a multitude of sins as well, according to God's Word. Yes, my husband and the "church" people were religious and put me in a box, but I was not loving or kind. Jesus/ Yeshua drew the sinners with love and kindness; then, they were healed due to His presence. I began to shut down because of the hurt I was experiencing instead of loving through it. God took me to His Word to show it to me, written in black and white. "Love is patient, love is kind. It does not envy, it does not boast, it is not proud. It does not dishonor others, it is not self-seeking, it is not easily angered; it keeps no record of wrongs. Love does not delight in evil but rejoices with the truth. It always protects, always trusts, always hopes, always perseveres." 1 Corinthians 13:4-7.

As I meditated on all of this, I realized that I had some changing to do, not just my husband. I had to allow God to walk me through the process, and it did not feel good at all. It is through love that true deliverance takes place. Why? Because God is love, and He alone delivers. Once I got into alignment with God's Word, my husband quickly lined up as well. I was surprised that all it took was for me to line up first to break the curse. You see, I was not just a curse breaker for him, but I needed one broken off me as well by him. We needed each other, and God, of course, to break free. When the curse broke, everyone that was no good for our marriage fell off as well. Today I can honestly thank all those that came against my marriage because it only pushed me deeper into God. I just love God so much for keeping me in His hands and opening my eyes to His ways. God truly knows best, and without Him, we are nothing. I felt like dying every day because our marriage's weight was heavy, but God did not allow it. It is a lot better to go through life with God on your side than without Him. He holds all the power and always delivers on His end. Also, I had to get back on the wall of prayer and to fight more strategically.

Prayer changes things because we serve a God who is alive and loves us enough to pull us out of a mess.

As women, we have an assignment added to our lives once we say, "I do," and that is to cover our husbands in pray and with love no matter what. If you do not remember anything from this book, remember Love covers. Love will push you to pray for results. If we love our husband, we are to cover him in pray even when he is out of order. Cover him even when he gets on your nerves or even when he mistreats you. I allowed my emotions to distract me, meanwhile leaving my husband uncovered. The enemy wants to take out the head of the family because he is the most vital link. The head is the covering that protects the family. Once the head is gone, or out of position, the rest of the family is neutralized. After a while, the rollercoaster ride I was on in my marriage consumed me, and I stopped giving my husband the love I owed him. Romans 13:8 states, "Let no debt remain outstanding, except the continuing debt to love one another, for whoever loves others has fulfilled the law." God commands us to love each other because that is what we owe to each other. It is not just a four-letter word to God! He values love so much so that He gave up His only Son for us. Love is an action word that requires dedication. When we follow God's Word, we follow Him because, according to John 1:1, the Word is God. Follow God in everything because He will not lead us astray.

Encouragement: Testimony of Overcoming

Let us fast forward four years down the road to December 2020. The curse is broken in Jesus/ Yeshua's name! The enemy thought he had us, but God stepped in and made a way out of no way. My husband and I are STILL married and are HAPPY! It took some work, but we were both willing to work at it. It all had to start at home. We made progress in a short time. I am pleased to announce that our marriage is growing stronger each day, and we have also become best friends. I thought that would never happen because his last best friend did not want to let him go, but all things are possible with God. Without God stepping into our marriage, we would have never made it. People would ask me why I got married, and how am I still married? My answer is simple, GOD. God is my answer and THE answer to everything. God honors marriage; therefore, it will work out for His glory if HE put the two together. We submitted to God and each other so God could get the glory out of our marriage. God had to strip us of everything and everyone for us to become one. He did not want anything to hinder our process any longer.

We had to go through homelessness, no money, no support, and almost losing our minds. God would send a person from time to time to help us when He saw we wanted to give up. We went through so much, but it was necessary. Looking back on it all, I would not change anything because God was with us every step of the way. I realized my shoes were only made for me, even if others wish they had access to them. The process made us more mature and able to identify where we needed work. Now we can recognize when other marriages are going through what we overcame. God enabled us to start a ministry, outreach organization, and multiple businesses. He even added three beautiful children to our family, making it five children altogether. We lost two children to miscarriages during our process, so to have five now all together is a blessing. I am grateful to God that we were still able to produce even in our process's wilderness stage. Some people cannot even grow in the promise stage of their life. Even when God could have left us, He did not. Even when people wanted God to turn away from us, He did not. We must trust God because He knows what He is doing. I will repeat; God knows best. We must become sold out for Him and His ways, no matter what it looks like or how it feels. I know we tend to stray away from God's process because we do not understand, but in due time we will. I was once there where you are, and I am fighting every day to keep the faith.

Just know you are not alone because God is with you. He honored you when you said, "I do," so He will fight for you. "For the Lord your God is the one who goes with you to fight for you against your enemies to give you victory." Deuteronomy 20:4.

"What, then, shall we say in response to these things? If God is for us, who can be against us? Romans 8:31. Stay humble, open to God, and in the posture of prayer. At the appointed time, God releases what He has in store for us and who He created us to be.

In conclusion, there is no such thing as a First Lady or a manual to teach you how to become one. However, there is such a thing as a Godly wife. A Godly wife is the wife God wants you to be, and He has a set way of how it should be executed. God values marriage, and He laid its foundation out in the book of Ephesians of the Bible. Marriage is work, and it is not solely for pleasure. It is a full-time job that carries on 24/7. There will be ups and downs because you married for better or for worse. Remember that! There is and will always be a sacrifice because marriage is a Kingdom assignment put together by God. The enemy hates God-ordained unions, so he will start chaos to get you distracted and wanting to give up. Home is the secret place where you get equipped and put into practice all you have learned.

Ladies just know it takes an extraordinary woman to walk beside her husband in a world that hates her. Keep showing up because God created YOU for the position!

Serenity Prayer

God grant me the serenity

to accept the things I cannot change;

courage to change the things I can;

and wisdom to know the difference.

Living one day at a time;

Enjoying one moment at a time;

Accepting hardships as the pathway to peace;

Taking, as He did, this sinful world

as it is, not as I would have it;

Trusting that He will make all things right

if I surrender to His Will;

That I may be reasonably happy in this life

and supremely happy with Him

Forever in the next.

Amen.

www.ingramcontent.com/pod-product-compliance
Lightning Source LLC
Chambersburg PA
CBHW071507080526
44587CB00016B/2719